What Did I

Fractions, Decimals, and Percents

Aubrie Nielsen

Consultants

Pamela Dase, M.A.Ed.
National Board Certified Teacher

Barbara Talley, M.S.
Texas A&M University

Publishing Credits

Dona Herweck Rice, *Editor-in-Chief*
Robin Erickson, *Production Director*
Lee Aucoin, *Creative Director*
Timothy J. Bradley, *Illustration Manager*
Sara Johnson, M.S.Ed., *Senior Editor*
Aubrie Nielsen, M.S.Ed., *Associate Education Editor*
Jennifer Kim, M.A.Ed., *Associate Education Editor*
Neri Garcia, *Senior Designer*
Stephanie Reid, *Photo Editor*
Rachelle Cracchiolo, M.S.Ed., *Publisher*

Image Credits

Teacher Created Materials

5301 Oceanus Drive
Huntington Beach, CA 92649-1030
http://www.tcmpub.com

ISBN 978-1-4333-3452-8

© 2012 Teacher Created Materials, Inc.

Table of Contents

What's in My Lunch?

I love food! I enjoy eating international foods like sushi, curries, and tamales. I am an adventurous eater and I love to try new foods. But I also like pizza, hamburgers, and candy! Sometimes I wonder exactly what is in the foods that I like to eat.

Today my swim team had a barbecue lunch to celebrate the end of our season. Everyone brought plenty of food to share. I helped grill the hot dogs. Once all the hot dogs were cooked, I helped myself to one. I also had some jello and a can of cola.

All of my teammates invited their families to attend the barbecue. Forty people came, so we had a lot of food.

Mole (moh-LAY) is a sauce used in Mexican cuisine (kwi-ZEEN).

Chicken tikka (TEE-kuh) masala (muh-SAH-luh) is a popular Indian dish.

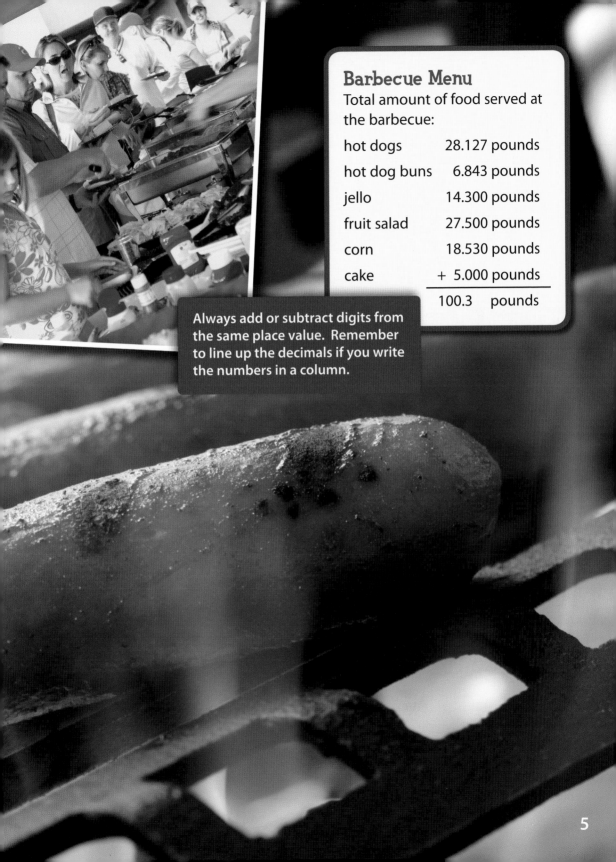

Barbecue Menu

Total amount of food served at the barbecue:

hot dogs	28.127 pounds
hot dog buns	6.843 pounds
jello	14.300 pounds
fruit salad	27.500 pounds
corn	18.530 pounds
cake	+ 5.000 pounds
	100.3 pounds

Always add or subtract digits from the same place value. Remember to line up the decimals if you write the numbers in a column.

What's in My Hot Dog?

I know what I like to put on my hot dog—ketchup, mustard, and onions! But what is in my hot dog? I decided to learn what makes up a hot dog.

It turns out there are many different types of hot dogs, including all-beef hot dogs, turkey hot dogs, and vegetarian hot dogs made from tofu.

The ingredients in my hot dog include beef, pork, water, salt, and something called "mechanically-separated turkey." I learned that mechanically-separated turkey has a soft texture, like paste. It is made by pushing turkey—including the bones—through a sieve (SIV). My hot dog also contains corn syrup, and several ingredients that are hard to pronounce! I never knew there were so many ingredients in a hot dog.

Tofu is made from soy milk. The soy milk is curdled and pressed into soft white blocks. Tofu comes from China and is widely used in Asian cuisine. It has a very mild taste, and can easily be flavored.

A package of hot dog buns weighs around 1 pound (453.6 grams). At the barbecue, there were 7 packages of hot dog buns. How many grams of hot dog buns were there?

$$
\begin{array}{r}
453.6 \\
453.6 \\
453.6 \\
453.6 \\
453.6 \\
453.6 \\
+\ 453.6 \\
\hline
3{,}175.2 \text{ grams}
\end{array}
\qquad \text{OR} \qquad
\begin{array}{r}
453.6 \\
\times\ 7 \\
\hline
3{,}175.2 \text{ grams}
\end{array}
$$

Decimal Places

Did you notice that there is one digit after the decimal place in the product of 453.6 and 7? That is because there is a total of one digit after the decimal place in the numbers that were multiplied.

A hot dog weighs 45 grams. About 1 **percent** (1%) of a hot dog is sodium. To find the portion that is sodium, use the following expression: 45 × 0.01 (0.01 is **equivalent** to 1%. To change a percent to a decimal, divide by 100. This moves the decimal point two places to the left.)

Multiplying Decimals

Step 1: Remove the decimals. Multiply.   45 × 1 = 45

Step 2: Count the number of decimal places in the **factors**.   45 × 0.<u>01</u>
    (2 decimal places)

Step 3: Place the decimal point in the product.   0.45

Portion that is sodium: 45 × 0.01 = 0.45 gram

meat being processed at a factory

LET'S EXPLORE MATH

a. The fruit salad at the team barbecue had 4,082.4 grams of strawberries, 2,721.6 grams of grapes, and 2,313.36 grams of pineapple. How many grams of fruit were in the fruit salad?

b. Next year, we plan to bring twice as much corn and three times as much jello for the barbecue. That is almost 50 more pounds of food! Use the information on page 5 to find how much of these items we will bring next year.

What's in My Jello?

Jello is fun to eat. I love all of its different colors and flavors and its unique texture. But what exactly is in this jiggly dessert?

My grandpa makes jello often. I have watched him dissolve the packet of powder in hot water, then pour it into a pan and place it in the refrigerator to chill. I wonder what is in the powder that combines with water to make such a colorful, wiggly treat.

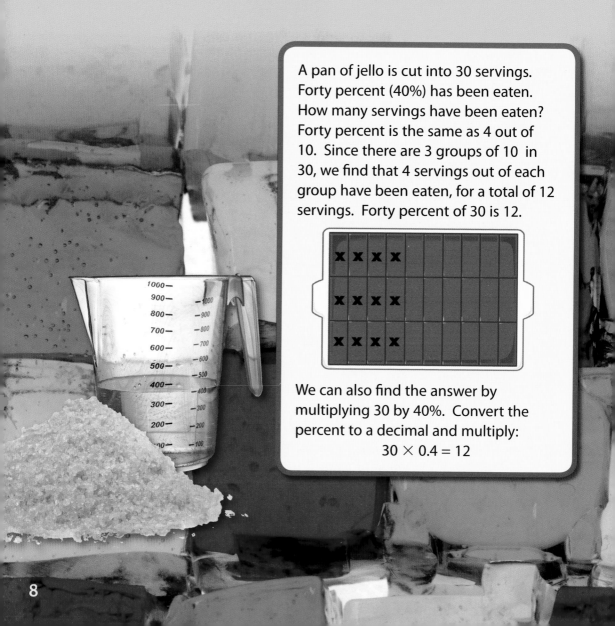

A pan of jello is cut into 30 servings. Forty percent (40%) has been eaten. How many servings have been eaten? Forty percent is the same as 4 out of 10. Since there are 3 groups of 10 in 30, we find that 4 servings out of each group have been eaten, for a total of 12 servings. Forty percent of 30 is 12.

We can also find the answer by multiplying 30 by 40%. Convert the percent to a decimal and multiply:

$$30 \times 0.4 = 12$$

I learned that gelatin (JEL-uh-tn) is what gives jello its texture. Gelatin is used in many food items that have a chewy or jelly-like texture, such as jelly, gummy candies, and marshmallows. It is also used in some cosmetics. Gelatin is made from collagen (KOL-uh-juhn). The collagen in gelatin comes from animal bones and hooves.

I noticed that my teammate Tejal didn't have any jello at our swim team barbecue. Tejal is a vegetarian. Many vegetarians choose not to eat foods made with gelatin, since it comes from animals.

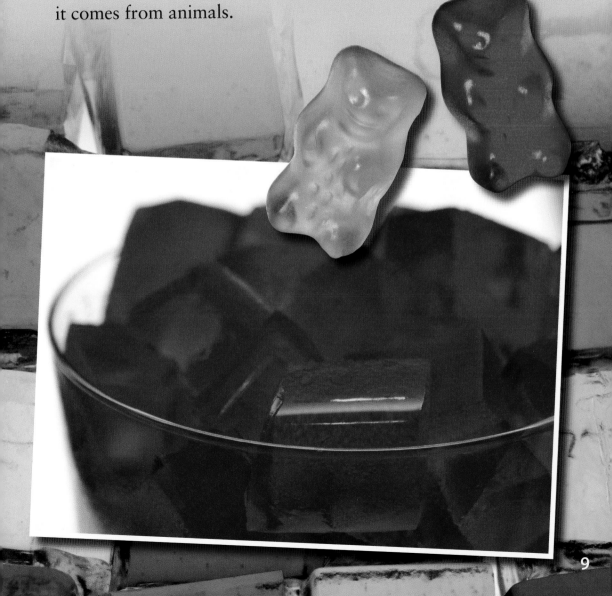

What's in My Cola?

It is a warm day, so I'm glad I have a cold can of cola to drink. I usually have milk or water with my meals at home, but once in a while, I pour myself a glass of fizzy cola. The first ingredient in my cola is carbonated (KAHR-buh-neyt-id) water. I learned that carbonated water is made by dissolving carbon dioxide gas into water. This makes the cola effervescent (ef-er-VES-uhnt), or bubbly.

The second ingredient is high fructose corn syrup. This makes the cola sweet. High fructose corn syrup is made from corn, and is used in place of sugar to sweeten many products because it is cheaper than sugar.

What Are Calories?
A calorie is a unit of energy. The energy we get from food is measured in calories. People need a certain number of calories each day to stay healthy.

A can of Sugar-Lite Cola has 98.2 calories. A can of Sugar-Plus Cola has 30% more calories than a can of Sugar-Lite Cola. Follow the steps to find the number of calories in Sugar-Plus Cola. Problems **a** and **b** use one method for finding a percent increase. Problem **c** uses a second method.

a. Find 98.2 x 0.3. This is the difference (in calories) in the two colas.

b. Add your answer for problem **a** to 98.2 to find the calories in Sugar-Plus Cola.

c. Multiply 98.2 by 1.3 to find the number of calories in Sugar-Plus Cola. (*Hint:* A 30% increase is the same as 130% of the original amount.)

d. Your answers for problems **b** and **c** should be the same. Explain why these answers are the same.

e. A third kind of cola has 48% more calories than Sugar-Lite Cola. How many calories does it have? Round to the nearest hundredth.

Coloring and flavoring are also added to my cola, along with **caffeine** (ka-FEEN).

Caffeine can give you a boost of energy. Some caffeine is considered safe, but too much can cause headaches, sleeplessness, and even anxiety (ang-ZAHY-i-tee). Most cola companies make a caffeine-free version of their cola for people who like the flavor of cola but don't want the caffeine.

Caffeine

Caffeine comes from coffee beans and tea leaves. It can also be found in the seeds, leaves, and fruits of some plants. It is not poisonous for humans, but it works as a **pesticide** (PES-tuh-sahyd) to paralyze or kill some insects that try to eat the plants.

Dinner at Aidan's House

After the barbecue, I went over to my teammate Aidan's house. His family invited me to stay for dinner. Aidan's family pays close attention to what they eat because Aidan has type 1 diabetes (dahy-uh-BEE-teez).

Aidan explained to me once that our bodies' cells need sugar that comes from our food. Many foods contain **carbohydrates** (kahr-boh-HAHY-dreyts), which our bodies break down into forms of sugar. Those sugars need some way to get into our cells. Insulin (IN-suh-lin) acts as a key to allow sugar to get into our cells. Insulin is a hormone made by our bodies.

Since Aidan has type 1 diabetes, his body does not make enough insulin. His white blood cells destroy his insulin-making cells.

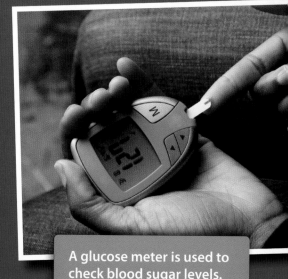

A glucose meter is used to check blood sugar levels.

These foods are especially rich in carbohydrates.

Different Types of Diabetes

There are different kinds of diabetes. Only about 5% of people with diabetes have type 1 diabetes. Type 1 diabetes is usually **diagnosed** in children and young adults. Type 2 diabetes is the most common form of the disease, and it affects people of all ages. **Obesity** and a lack of physical activity are major factors in the onset of type 2 diabetes.

Aidan has had type 1 diabetes for 6.25 years (six years and three months). He tests his blood sugar about eight times per day. That means he has tested his blood sugar about 8 × 6.25 × 365 times. That is 18,250 blood tests!

Since his body does not produce insulin, Aidan must take insulin every day. He gives himself about four insulin injections per day. That means he has given himself about 4 × 6.25 × 365, or 9,125 injections. He hopes that a cure will be found someday.

insulin

insulin molecule

LET'S EXPLORE MATH

To stay healthy, doctors recommend that most people consume 271 grams of carbohydrates each day. Leila has diabetes. Her doctor recommends that she consume 52% fewer carbohydrates per day.

a. How many fewer grams of carbohydrates must Leila eat each day?

b. How many grams of carbohydrates can Leila eat each day?

c. If Leila had to eat 70% fewer grams of carbohydrates, how many grams of carbohydrates could she eat each day?

Aidan's family made spaghetti for dinner. It was so delicious that we both cleaned our plates. Aidan had to determine the amount of carbohydrates that he had eaten so he could give himself the correct amount of insulin. He used the nutrition facts on the spaghetti sauce label to show me how he made his determination.

Aidan explained that spaghetti sauce, like other foods, is made up of **nutrients** (NOO-tree-uhnts). These nutrients include fat, carbohydrates, protein, water, vitamins, and minerals.

Nutrition Facts

Serving size: 1 cup

Fat	1.200 grams
Carbohydrate	11.268 grams
Protein	3.032 grams
Water	106.300 grams
Other	3.400 grams
Total	125.2 grams

Aidan first showed me what percentage of the sauce is carbohydrate. He reminded me that 11.268 out of 125.2 grams of the sauce is made up of carbohydrate. He told me to divide 11.268 by 125.2. I did and found the quotient to be 0.09. When I changed 0.09 to a percent, I found that 9% of the sauce is carbohydrate.

$$125.2\,\overline{)11\,2.68}$$
$$\quad 0.09$$
$$-11\,2\,68$$
$$\qquad\quad 0$$

Notice that we move the decimal in both the **divisor** and the **dividend** so that we can divide by a whole number.

$100 \times 0.09 = 9\%$

Converting a Decimal to a Percent

Moving the decimal point two places to the right is the same as multiplying by 100. When we change a decimal to a percent, we are showing what part of 100 it is.

Tomatoes are a basic ingredient in spaghetti sauce. Once thought to be poisonous, the tomato is now a widely popular fruit. There are thousands of varieties.

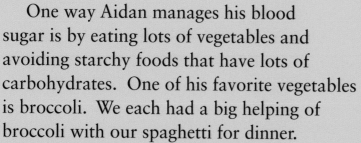

One way Aidan manages his blood sugar is by eating lots of vegetables and avoiding starchy foods that have lots of carbohydrates. One of his favorite vegetables is broccoli. We each had a big helping of broccoli with our spaghetti for dinner.

Aidan knows a lot about broccoli! He told me that broccoli has twice as much vitamin C as an orange, and almost as much calcium as a glass of milk. It is also full of antioxidants (an-tee-OK-si-duhnts), which help prevent diseases like cancer and heart disease.

Foods rich in antioxidants include green tea, pistachios, cranberries, avocados, tomatoes, lentils, and even dark chocolate!

Recommended Dietary Allowances

The Food and Nutrition Board of the Institute of Medicine publishes guidelines for how many nutrients and calories people need each day to stay healthy. One of these guidelines is called the Recommended Dietary Allowances (RDA). The RDA is a goal for average daily intake based on a diet of 2,000 calories per day.

LET'S EXPLORE MATH

a. Look at the nutrition label for a serving of spaghetti sauce on page 14. What percent of a serving of sauce is water? What percent of a serving of sauce is protein? Round your answers to the nearest tenth of a percent.

b. A serving of broccoli has 6 grams of carbohydrates. The Recommended Dietary Allowance of carbohydrates is 130 grams. What percent of the RDA of carbohydrates is in one serving of broccoli? Round your answer to the nearest tenth of a percent.

A single serving of broccoli has all of the vitamin C a person needs in one day. In fact, it has 135 percent of the RDA. Aidan told me that most dark green vegetables are very high in vitamins and nutrients. I really like vegetables, so it's great to know that they are filled with so many things that my body needs.

Omelets for Breakfast

My family really enjoys cooking, so we try to make breakfast together every weekend. After learning about the health benefits of vegetables from Aidan, I wanted to make a breakfast that was filled with veggies. I found a recipe for omelets that we decided to try this morning.

The omelet recipe calls for $1\frac{1}{2}$ cups of onions, $2\frac{3}{4}$ cups of bell peppers, and $1\frac{5}{8}$ cups of mushrooms.

To find the total amount of these ingredients in the omelet, add the mixed numbers.

Step 1: Find a common denominator. Make it the **least common denominator (LCD)** if possible

$$1\frac{1}{2} + 2\frac{3}{4} + 1\frac{5}{8}$$
$$1\frac{}{8} + 2\frac{}{8} + 1\frac{}{8}$$

Step 2: Find equivalent fractions.

$$1\frac{4}{8} + 2\frac{6}{8} + 1\frac{5}{8}$$

Step 3: Add the whole numbers and add the fractions. Remember that when adding fractions, add only the numerators. The denominators stay the same.

$$4\frac{15}{8}$$

Step 4: Simplify the **improper fraction**. Divide the numerator by the denominator to get a mixed number.

$$4 + 1\frac{7}{8}$$

Step 5: Add the whole numbers and write the final answer as a mixed number.

$$5\frac{7}{8} \text{ cups}$$

Finding the Least Common Denominator (LCD)

First, list **multiples** of each different denominator. Stop when you find a multiple that they all share. This is your LCD.

2: 2, 4, 6, ⑧

4: 4, ⑧

8: ⑧

The first step in the recipe is to **sauté** (saw-TEY) the onions and green peppers in butter. I cooked the vegetables until they were tender, which took about five minutes. While the veggies were cooking, I beat the eggs with some milk in a separate bowl. I added salt, pepper, and a few other herbs for flavor. One of my favorite parts of cooking is being creative with recipes and adding unique ingredients.

A mushroom is actually a **fungus**, not a vegetable. A fungus differs from a vegetable in that it does not have leaves, roots, or seeds, and it does not need light to grow.

LET'S EXPLORE MATH

a. I added three herbs to the omelets: $1\frac{1}{3}$ teaspoons of oregano, $1\frac{1}{4}$ teaspoons of thyme, and $\frac{1}{8}$ teaspoon of sage. How many teaspoons of herbs did I add in all?

b. The recipe called for $1\frac{1}{4}$ teaspoons of salt, but I decided to reduce the salt by $\frac{2}{3}$ teaspoon. How much salt did I put in the omelets?

My sister helped grate the cheese while I cooked the eggs. Once the eggs were cooked, my sister sprinkled on the cheese and spooned the cooked vegetables into the middle of the omelet. Then I folded over the omelet and cooked it for a few minutes longer to melt the cheese. It is challenging to successfully flip the omelet so it can cook on both sides. I slid it onto a plate and started on the next omelet.

Simplifying Fractions

To simplify a fraction, divide the numerator and the denominator by their **greatest common factor (GCF)**. When a fraction is in **simplest form**, the GCF of the numerator and denominator is 1.

We decided to put a mix of different cheeses in the omelets. The recipe called for $\frac{3}{4}$ pound of cheese. We decided to make $\frac{2}{3}$ of that cheddar cheese. How much of the cheese was cheddar?

cc	cc	cc	
cc	cc	cc	

cc = cheddar cheese

We multiplied the fractions to find that we needed $\frac{1}{2}$ pound of cheddar cheese.

$$\frac{2}{3} \times \frac{3}{4} = \frac{2 \times 3}{3 \times 4} = \frac{6}{12}$$

Simplify: $\frac{6}{12} \div \frac{2}{2} = \frac{1}{2}$

One recipe for salsa calls for $\frac{3}{4}$ cup of onions.

a. How much onion is needed for half the recipe?

b. How much onion is needed for a double recipe?

c. How much onion is needed to increase the recipe $2\frac{1}{2}$ times?

d. Add your answer from problem **a** to your answer from problem **b**. How does this sum compare with your answer to problem **c**?

My family likes to put salsa on our omelets. Salsa is one of my mom's specialties. She has made it so often that she doesn't need to use a recipe. She starts by crushing tomatoes, then adding some chopped chiles, onions, garlic, and cilantro.

My mom made 30 ounces of salsa. $\frac{5}{6}$ of the salsa is tomatoes. How many ounces of tomatoes are in the salsa? $\frac{5}{6}$ of 30 is 25. There are 25 ounces of tomatoes in the salsa.

$$30 \times \frac{5}{6} = \frac{30}{1} \times \frac{5}{6} = \frac{30 \times 5}{1 \times 6} = \frac{150}{6} = 25$$

We invited my aunt, uncle, and cousins over for breakfast, and I made omelets for everyone. We sat together at the table and passed the salsa around. By the time it got to me, $\frac{5}{6}$ of the salsa was left. I needed to make sure there would be enough for my sister and three cousins to have some, too, so I divided $\frac{5}{6}$ by five and found that we could each have $\frac{1}{6}$ of the remaining salsa.

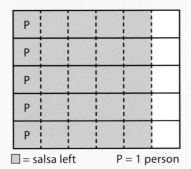

□ = salsa left   P = 1 person

$\frac{5}{6} \div 5$ is the same as $\frac{5}{6} \div \frac{5}{1}$

Step 1: Multiply by the **reciprocal**. $\frac{5}{6} \times \frac{1}{5} = \frac{5}{30}$

Step 2: Simplify. $\frac{5}{30} \div \frac{5}{5} = \frac{1}{6}$

Notice that dividing by 5 is equivalent to multiplying by $\frac{1}{5}$.

Fruit or Vegetable?

Many people are confused about whether a tomato is a fruit or a vegetable. A tomato is scientifically a fruit because it develops from a flower and contains the seeds of the plant. Many people think of it as a vegetable because it is not as sweet as other fruits. Cucumbers, zucchini, squash, avocados, peppers, peas, and pumpkins are other fruits that many people consider to be vegetables.

We had milk to drink with our breakfast. Milk is high in calcium, which helps build strong bones and teeth. It also has protein, which is a source of energy, and plenty of other vitamins and nutrients. Lowfat milk only has 102 calories per serving, and is part of a healthy diet.

We had $1\frac{1}{4}$ gallons of milk. One serving of milk is $\frac{1}{16}$ of a gallon. How many servings of milk did we have?

Each bar is divided into sixteenths to show the serving size. We are looking for the number of $\frac{1}{16}$-servings in $1\frac{1}{4}$ gallons of milk. Notice that $1\frac{1}{4}$ bars are shaded. Count the $\frac{1}{16}$-servings to see that there are 20 servings.

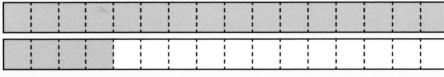

$$1\frac{1}{4} \div \frac{1}{16} = 1\frac{1}{4} \times \frac{16}{1} = \frac{5}{4} \times \frac{16}{1} = \frac{80}{4} = 20$$

Notice that dividing by $\frac{1}{16}$ is equivalent to multiplying by 16.

Milk is 85–95% water. The creamy texture comes from the 5–15% that is vitamins, proteins, carbohydrates, and fat.

Improper Fractions

To simplify an improper fraction, divide the numerator by the denominator. You may get a whole number or a mixed number. If you get a mixed number, remember to simplify the fraction.

Thinking About Food

I have never thought much about what I eat before. It has been interesting to analyze my meals over the last couple of days. I was surprised about some of the ingredients in things that I eat, and I plan to look at nutrition labels more often in the future. It is important to think about what you eat so you can be sure you are making healthy choices and getting the nutrients your body needs. After your next meal, try asking yourself, *what did I eat?*

Nutrition Facts Labels

Many countries require packaged foods to be labeled with nutrition facts. These labels give information about the amount of calories and nutrients in the product based on the serving size. Pay close attention to the serving size! Even products that seem to be packaged as single servings may have nutrition facts based on smaller portions.

a. How many $\frac{1}{4}$-cup servings are in 3 cups of frozen yogurt?

b. How many $1\frac{3}{4}$-pound portions are in a $5\frac{1}{2}$-pound bag of rice?

c. How many $\frac{5}{12}$-ounce servings are in $\frac{7}{8}$ ounce of cheese?

from Fat   260
                            80

% Daily Val

Total Fat 9g *   14%   26

Saturated Fat 3.5g   18%   30

Cholesterol 0mg   0%   1%

Sodium 360mg   15%   20%

Total Carbohydrate 46g 15%   15%   16%

Dietary Fiber 1g

Sugars 28g   4%   4%

tein 2g

min A

in C

PROBLEM-SOLVING ACTIVITY

The Chip Factory

Factories must make sure that the food they produce is free of **contamination** (kuhn-tam-uh-NEY-shuhn), like insects and mold. They also must make sure that the food tastes correct. They check that it is the right size and color. Samples of the product are tested for quality.

At a potato chip factory, four bags of potato chips are pulled aside from each batch for testing. Each bag weighs 1.2 ounces.

Solve It!

a. All four bags of chips are mixed together to make a large sample. How much does the sample weigh?

b. The large sample is then divided into six smaller samples. How much does each of the six samples weigh?

c. Two-thirds of the samples are original flavor. What is the weight of the samples that are original flavor?

d. If the potato chip factory produces 100 bags of chips per batch, what is the percent of bags in each batch that are not tested?

Use the steps below to help solve the problems.

Step 1: Use repeated addition or multiplication to find the total weight of four bags of chips.

Step 2: Divide your answer for problem **a** by 6.

Step 3: Multiply your answer for problem **a** by $\frac{2}{3}$.

Step 4: Subtract the number of bags tested from the number of bags of potato chips produced. Write a fraction that shows the number of bags not tested over the total number of bags in the batch. Change the fraction to a decimal by dividing, then multiply by 100.

Glossary

caffeine—a bitter substance found in coffee, tea, cocoa, and some colas

carbohydrates—substances found in some foods that provide our bodies with heat and energy, and are made from carbon, hydrogen, and oxygen

contamination—the introduction of a material that does not belong

curdled—thickened and separated into solids and liquids

diagnosed—identified or recognized as having a disease or illness

dividend—a number to be divided

divisor—a number by which another number is divided

equivalent—having the same value

factors—numbers that divide exactly into another number; numbers multiplied together to get a product

fungus—a plant that has no flower and lives on dead or decaying things

greatest common factor (GCF)—the largest factor shared by two numbers

improper fraction— a fraction whose numerator is greater than its denominator, for example $\frac{40}{2}$

least common denominator (LCD)—the smallest common multiple of the denominators of two or more fractions

multiples—products of a whole number and any other whole number

nutrients—substances that plants, animals, and people need to live and grow

obesity—the condition of being very overweight

percent—a part of a whole expressed in hundredths

pesticide—a chemical that is used to kill animals or insects that damage plants or crops

reciprocal—either of a pair of numbers (such as $\frac{2}{3}$ and $\frac{3}{2}$) whose product is 1

sauté—to fry in a small amount of fat

sieve—a tool that has many small holes and is used to separate small pieces from larger pieces, or solids from liquids

simplest form—a fraction whose numerator and denominator have no common factor greater than 1

Index

Let's Explore Math

Page 7:
a. 9,117.36 grams
b. corn: 37.06 pounds; jello: 42.9 pounds

Page 11:
a. 29.46 calories
b. 127.66 calories
c. 127.66 calories
d. The answers are the same because a 30% increase in calories is the same as 130% of the original calories (30% = 0.3 and 130% = 1.3).
e. 145.34 calories

Page 13:
a. 140.92 grams
b. 130.08 grams
c. 81.3 grams

Page 17:
a. water: 84.9%; protein: 2.4%
b. 4.6%

Page 19:
a. $2\frac{17}{24}$ teaspoons
b. $\frac{7}{12}$ teaspoon

Page 21:
a. $\frac{3}{8}$ cup
b. $1\frac{1}{2}$ cups
c. $1\frac{7}{8}$ cups
d. $1\frac{7}{8}$ cups; The answers are the same.

Page 27:
a. 12 servings
b. $3\frac{1}{7}$ portions
c. $2\frac{1}{10}$ servings

Problem-Solving Activity

a. 4.8 ounces
b. 0.8 ounce
c. 3.2 ounces
d. 96%